Dr Sebi's Plant-Based Healing Meals

Dr Sebi's Full Plant-Based Diet Guide with 50 Easy Recipes and Liver Cleansing, Weight Loss Food List

By

Spoons of Happiness

The information provided herein is stated to be truthful and consistent, in that any liability, in terms of inattention or otherwise, by any usage or abuse of any policies, processes, or directions contained within is the solitary and utter responsibility of the recipient reader. Under no circumstances will any legal responsibility or blame be held against the publisher for any reparation, damages, or monetary loss due to the information herein, either directly or indirectly.

Respective authors own all copyrights not held by the publisher.

The information herein is offered for informational purposes solely, and is universal as so. The presentation of the information is without contract or any type of guarantee assurance.

The trademarks that are used are without any consent, and the publication of the trademark is without permission or backing by the trademark owner. All trademarks and brands within this book are for clarifying purposes only and are the owned by the owners themselves, not affiliated with this document.

Table of Contents

Introduction

The Dr Sebi diet, also called the "Dr Sebi alkaline diet," is an herbal diet developed by the late Dr Sebi. It is said to rejuvenate cells by eliminating toxic waste by alkalinizing the blood.

The diet is based on eating a short list of approved foods along with many supplements.

This particular diet is founded on the African theory of bio-mineral balance and was first developed by Alfredo Darrington Bowman, a self-taught herbalist, also known as Dr Sebi. Regardless of his name, Dr Sebi wasn't actually a medical doctor, and he did not own a Ph.D.

He designed this diet for anyone who wants to cure or prevent disease naturally and improve their overall health without relying on conventional Western medicine.

According to Dr Sebi, the disease is the result of a buildup of mucus in one area of your body. For example, a buildup of mucus in the lungs is pneumonia, while excess mucus in the pancreas is diabetes.

He reasons that these diseases are not able to exist in an alkaline environment and start to develop when your body gets too acidic.

By strictly following his diet and using his expensive patented supplements, he promises to restore your body's natural alkaline state and detoxify your ailing body.

Originally, Dr Sebi asserted that this diet was capable of curing conditions such as AIDS, leukemia, sickle cell anemia, and lupus. However, after a 1993 lawsuit, he was ordered to stop making such claims.

The diet is a specific list of approved veggies, fruits, grains, seeds, nuts, oils, and herbs.

Sebi stated that in order for his body to heal itself, he must follow the diet consistently for the rest of his life.

Chapter 1. Salads Recipes

1. Coleslaw

(Ready in about 15 minutes | Serving 4| Difficulty: Easy)

Per serving: Kcal 140, Fat: 8g, Net Carbs: 8g, Protein: 10g

Ingredients:

For the salad

- 3 cups finely chopped cabbage
- 1 carrot, finely chopped
- ½ red bell pepper, diced
- ¼ cup dill pickles, diced

For the Dressing

- 3 tablespoons vinegar
- 1 tablespoon agave
- 2 tablespoons nondairy milk
- 4 tablespoons Green Garden Mayonnaise
- ½ teaspoon dill
- ½ teaspoon celery seed
- Sea salt and black pepper to taste

Directions:

1. In a cup, combine the cabbage, carrot, red pepper, and dill pickles.

2. Mix the vinegar, agave, yogurt, mayonnaise, dill, and celery seeds in a separate cup.

3. Mix the cabbage, carrot, red pepper, and dill pickles with the dressing.

4. Add black pepper and salt.

2. Fresh tomato and Avacado Pasta Salad

(Ready in about 25 minutes | Serving 8| Difficulty: Easy)

Per serving: Kcal 140, Fat: 8g, Net Carbs: 8g, Protein: 10g

Ingredients:

- 3 cups whole wheat pasta shells, cooked

- ¼ cup diced red onions

- 2½ cups cherry tomatoes, quartered

- 1 15-ounce can chickpeas, drained and rinsed

- ½ cup basil leaves, finely chopped

- 2 avocados, diced

- 1½ cups cooked corn

- ¼ cup Green Garden Mayonnaise

- Sea salt to taste

Directions:

1. Cook pasta according to the instructions for the kit.

2. Combine the onions, tomatoes, chickpeas, basil, avocado, and maize in a large bowl. Add the cooked pasta and mayonnaise, and season with salt.

3. Refrigerate and serve cold.

3. Greek Salad with Nuts

(Ready in about25 minutes | Serving 8| Difficulty: Easy)

Per serving: Kcal 140, Fat: 8g, Net Carbs: 8g, Protein: 10g

Ingredients:

For the Salads

- 6 cups salad greens

- 1 red onion, diced

- 1 red bell pepper, seeded and diced

- ½ cup cherry tomatoes, quartered

- 1 large cucumber, sliced

- ¼ cup chopped black olives

- ¼-½ cup pine nuts or chopped walnuts

For the Dressing

- ½ block extra firm tofu, crumbled
- ½ cup red wine vinegar
- 2 teaspoons lemon juice
- ½ teaspoon salt
- 1 teaspoon oregano
- ¼ teaspoon thyme
- ¼ teaspoon black pepper

Directions:

1. In a large salad bowl, combine the salad greens, onion, pepper, tomatoes, cucumbers, olives, and nuts.

2. Mix all the ingredients in a bowl for dressing and allow the tofu to marinate for 1 hour.

3. Pour the dressing over the lettuce and toss to cover.

4. Lemon Tahini Quinoa Salad

(Ready in about 25 minutes | Serving 8| Difficulty: Easy)

Per serving: Kcal 140, Fat: 8g, Net Carbs: 8g, Protein: 10g

Ingredients:

For the salad

- 2 cups of water

- 1 cup quinoa, uncooked

- ½ red onion, finely diced

- 1 cup chopped broccoli

- 1 medium red bell pepper, seeded and diced

- 1 medium yellow bell pepper, seeded and diced

- 2 tomatoes, diced

- 1 15-ounce can chickpeas

For the sauce

- ¼ cup tahini

- 3 tablespoons fresh lemon juice

- 2 tablespoons hot water

- 2 tablespoons (low sodium) tamari

- 2 teaspoons sweetener

- 1 teaspoon powdered garlic

- Sea salt to taste

Directions:

1. Heat 2 cups of water and quinoa over high heat until boiling in a medium saucepan. Reduce heat to medium-low and simmer for about 15 minutes until water and quinoa fluff up is absorbed. Quinoa is finished when it's tender, and each bite has a pop. Drain the water and put the quinoa in a blender.

2. Add the cabbage, broccoli, peppers, chickpeas, and tomatoes.

3. Whisk together all the ingredients in order to make the sauce.

4. For cooked quinoa and vegetables, add the sauce.

5. Garnished with a little cilantro, serve.

5. Lettuce Wraps

(Ready in about 25 minutes | Serving 10|
Difficulty: Easy)

Per serving: Kcal 140, Fat: 8g, Net Carbs: 8g,
Protein: 10g

Ingredients:

- 1 head Bibb lettuce

- ½ cup vegetable broth

- 3 cloves garlic, minced

- 1 tablespoon diced fresh ginger

- ½ medium onion, diced

- 1 large carrot, grated or thinly sliced

- 1 celery stalk, finely chopped

- 1 cup water chestnuts, diced

- 2 tablespoons sesame seeds

- ¼ cup light soy sauce

- 2 cups cooked bulgur

- 2 tablespoons nutritional yeast

- 1 teaspoon thyme, dried leaves

- Sea salt and black pepper to taste

Peanut Dressing

- ¼ cup natural peanut butter

- 1 tablespoon soy sauce or tamari

- ½ teaspoon ginger, grated

- ¼ cup Mae Ploy

- ¼ cup coconut milk, lite

Directions:

1. Wash the leaves of the lettuce, pat them dry, and set aside.

2. Add the vegetable broth, garlic, ginger, onion, carrot, celery, and chestnuts to a medium skillet. Cook until the onion is translucent under medium-high pressure.

3. Sesame seeds, soy sauce, and bulgur are added. For 1-2 minutes, fry. Remove from heat, add nutritional yeast and thyme, and season with salt and pepper.

4. Whisk all the ingredients together for the peanut dressing.

5. Take a whole leaf of lettuce and add 2-3 tablespoons of filling in the center. Add 1 spoonful of peanut dressing. Roll into a wrap and enjoy.

Chapter 2. Smoothies and Drinks

6. All-Natural Tamarind Paste

To make a refreshing drink, this tamarind paste can be mixed with water or used as a seasoning to add a sweet and sour flavor to your dishes!

(Ready in 45-60 min, serve 3, Difficulty: Normal)

Per serving: Kcal 226.5, Fat: 0.8g, Net Carbs:12.6g, Protein: 13.5g

Ingredients:

- 250 gr of natural tamarind

- 3 cups of spring water

Directions:

1. Make the tamarind clean. Check for and discard any seeds, skin, or unwanted particles. Heat 2 cups of water, meanwhile.

2. For around 45-60 minutes, soak the tamarind in 2 cups of hot water.

3. Once the tamarind is soft, blend it until very smooth in a high-speed blender.

4. Move via a sifter with the resulting mixture. Throw away any rocks, seeds, or debris.

5. Boil the resulting pulp over a medium flame for 5 minutes.

6. Store in airtight containers until the paste is fully cooled.

7. Dr Sebi's Heavy Metal Detox Smoothie

Do you know the effects of the toxicity of heavy metals? The Heavy Metal Detox Smoothie from Dr Sebi is ideally formulated to include six main ingredients that work together to clean heavy metals from the organs they absorb in synergy.

(Ready in 10 min| serve 3| Difficulty: Normal)

Per serving: Kcal 226.5, Fat: 0.8g, Net Carbs:12.6g, Protein: 13.5g

Ingredients:

- 1 burro banana

- 1-2 cups blueberries

- 1 cup Seville orange juice

- 1 cup watercress

- 1 organic apple

- 1 tablespoon of Dr Sebi's Bromide Plus Powder

- 1 cup spring water

Directions:

1. Mix all ingredients in a high-speed blender until smooth to prepare the heavy metal detox smoothie.

2. Add up to 1 cup of water if a thinner consistency is needed.

3. Enjoy!

8. Dr Sebi's "Brain-Boosting" Smoothie

Now that you know the value of caring for the wellbeing of your brain, it's time for the "Brain-Boosting" Smoothie from Dr Sebi! Blueberries and raspberries are used in this Brain-Boosting Smoothie, which battles oxidative stress and free radical harm that triggers memory malfunctions. It also provides other ingredients to provide you with mental insight and an energy boost. Plus, it's yummy!

(Ready in 10-15 min| serve 3| Difficulty: Normal)

Per serving: Kcal 226.5, Fat: 0.8g, Net Carbs:12.6g, Protein: 13.5g

Ingredients:

- 1 cup of Dr Sebi's Nerve/Stress Relief Herbal Tea

- 1/2 cup of raspberries

- 1/2 cup blueberries

- 1/2 burro banana

- 1 tablespoon of date sugar or agave syrup

Directions:

1. To prepare your "brain-boosting" smoothie, start by boiling one cup of distilled water and add 1/2 tablespoon of Dr Sebi's Nerve / Stress Relief Herbal Tea.

2. Steep for 10 – 15 minutes, strain. Let cool.

3. Once the tea is cooled, blend in a high-speed blender along with the rest of the ingredients.

4. Enjoy!

9. Dr Sebi's "Blissful" Smoothie

The "Blissful" Smoothie from Dr Sebi is filled with avocados. These are rich in vitamin B to help keep healthy nerve cells and brain cells, and you are much happier. This smoothie gives you all of the quinoa's heartiness with very strong mental and physical health benefits and gives you a filling and appetizing drink.

(Ready in 10-15 min| serve 3| Difficulty: Normal)

Per serving: Kcal 226.5, Fat: 0.8g, Net Carbs:12.6g, Protein: 13.5g

Ingredients:

- 1 pear, chopped

- 1/4 avocado, pitted

- 1 oz. blueberries

- 1/4 cup cooked quinoa

- 1 cup water

Directions:

1. Mix all the ingredients in a high-speed blender to prepare your smoothie and enjoy it!

10. Dr Sebi's Detox Blueberry Smoothie

A berry-filled delight that will help your body get rid of accumulated toxins and keep your body clean and nourished from the inside out is Dr Sebi's Detox Berry Smoothie.

(Ready in 10-15 min| serve 3| Difficulty: Normal)

Per serving: Kcal 226.5, Fat: 0.8g, Net Carbs:12.6g, Protein: 13.5g

Ingredients:

- 1 medium burro banana

- 1 Seville orange

- 1 cup blueberries

- 2 cups fresh lettuce

- 1 tablespoon hemp seeds

- Water

- 1/4 avocado, pitted

Directions:

1. Add the water to your blender first, followed by the fruit and the greens.

2. Blend all ingredients until smooth and enjoy!

Chapter 3. Soup Recipes

11. Thai Vegetable Soup

(Ready in 20min| serve4-6| Difficulty: Normal)

Per serving: Kcal 226.5, Fat: 0.8g, Net Carbs: 12.6g, Protein: 13.5g

Ingredients:

- Coconut water from 3 young coconuts, or about 3½ cups of your favourite coconut water

- Coconut meat scraped from ½ coconut (about 4 to 6 ounces), optional

- 1 sweet potato, peeled and cut into 1½-inch pieces

- 2 yams, peeled and cut into 1½-inch pieces

- 1 small butternut squash, peeled, halved, seeded, and cubed

- 2 small carrots, peeled and diced

- ¼ pound shiitake or cremini mushrooms, sliced

- 2 medium tomatoes, diced

- 3 stalks of lemongrass (bottom white part only), halved and cut into 2-inch pieces

- 2 jalapeño peppers, halved and seeded

- 3 kaffir lime leaves

- ½ medium onion, peeled and diced

- 1-inch piece ginger, peeled and scored

- 2 cloves garlic, peeled and minced

- Juice from 2 large limes (about ½ cup)

- 1½ tablespoons low-sodium soy sauce

- 1½ teaspoons ground coriander

- Pinch white pepper

- 3 cups spinach (about ½ pound), coarsely chopped

- 1½ cups snow peas, trimmed

- Chopped cilantro

Directions:

1. In a blender, add the coconut water and coconut meat and puree on top.

2. Combine pureed coconut, sweet potato, yams, in a large stockpot, also carrots, mushrooms, tomatoes, lemongrass,

jalapeño squash, butternut squash, Kaffir, tomato, citrus leaves, cabbage, ginger, garlic, soy sauce, lime juice, Coriander, and pepper in white. Carry it over high heat to a boil. Reduce the amount of Simmer for 20 minutes and heat to medium-low. Add the lettuce and the spinach, Cook the snow peas for 1 minute.

3. Take the pot away from the heat. Remove and discard the ginger, lemongrass, Leaves of lime, and jalapeños. Garnish with cilantro and serve right away.

12. Tom Yum Goong (Thai Hot-and-Sour Soup)

(Ready in 20min| serve4| Difficulty: Normal)

Per serving: Kcal 226.5, Fat: 0.8g, Net Carbs: 12.6g, Protein: 13.5g

Ingredients:

- 4 cups Vegetable Stock or low-sodium vegetable broth

- 4 thin slices fresh ginger

- 1 stalk lemongrass, cut into 1-inch pieces

- 2 tablespoons Thai red curry paste

- 3 tablespoons low-sodium soy sauce

- Zest and juice of 2 limes

- 1 14-ounce can lite coconut milk

- 3 shallots, peeled and thinly sliced

- 2 Roma tomatoes, chopped

- 1 head baby bok choy, thinly sliced

- 1 small carrot, peeled and cut into matchsticks

- 1 cup mung bean sprouts

- ¼ cup chopped Thai basil

- 2 Thai red chiles, sliced into thin rounds

- Cilantro sprigs

Directions:

1. Add the vegetable reserve, ginger, lemongrass, curry paste, to a big saucepan, Soy sauce, juice and lime zest, and coconut milk. Bring the kettle to a boil over the mixture e elevated heat.

2. Add the shallots, onions, bok choy and carrot to the mixture. Reduce the heat to medium-low and simmer for about 25 minutes, until the vegetables are tender.

3. Drop the lemongrass and ginger and add the sprouts of mung beans, basil, and Chiles. Garnished with cilantro, serve.

13. Carrot and Ginger Soup Recipe

(Ready in about 40 minutes | Serving 2 | Difficulty: Easy)

Per serving: Kcal 255, Fat: 22g, Net Carbs: 37.4g, Protein: 8.8g

Ingredients:

For the Soup:

- 600g of carrots, peeled and chopped
- 2 medium onions, peeled and chopped
- 1 clove of garlic, peeled and crushed
- 3 tbsp olive oil
- 1 tsp powdered ginger
- 1 tsp medium curry powder
- 11/2 litres good stock, chicken or vegetable
- Sea salt and black pepper
- The pared rind of one lemon

For the Lemon Herb Cream, For Serving:

- 1 x 200g crème fraiche
- Finely grated rind of one lemon

- 2 tsp chopped parsley

- 2 tsp chopped chives

Directions:

1. In a saucepan, heat the olive oil, add the onions or carrots, and cook over several minutes, stirring periodically. Don't keep the veggies purple.

2. Then add the garlic, curry powder, and ginger and cook for another minute. Add to the pan the stock and lemon strips, half place the bowl with its lid, and boil gently until the carrots are soft for 20 minutes.

3. Slightly cool and then solubilize the soup until it is smooth with salt and black pepper, taste, and season. Reheat it for cooking.

4. For lemon herb cream: Blend all the ingredients and put on top of the soup with a spoonful.

14. Creamy Pea and Watercress Soup Recipe

(Ready in about 40 minutes | Serving 2 | Difficulty: Easy)

Per serving: Kcal 215, Fat: 20g, Net Carbs: 47.4g, Protein: 7.8g

Ingredients:

- 25g butter
- 1 onion, finely chopped
- 300g fresh or frozen peas, reserve 100g
- 100g or 2 bags watercress
- 1 large potato, peeled and cubed
- 1-liter vegetable stock
- A handful of fresh mint
- Salt and Black Pepper
- 60g natural bio yogurt
- Fresh mint, chopped to serve, optional

Directions:

1. In a saucepan, warm the butter and add the onion. Cook until translucent and smooth.

2. Add 200 g of the peas, cress, and potatoes and simmer till soft as well as wilted.

3. Insert the vegetable stock and then boil about 15-20 minutes, adding the last of peas, bringing extra vibrancy to the broth.

4. Add mint and seasoning, then blitz until smooth with a blender.

5. Scatter with fresh mint in warm bowls and then spoon with yogurt.

15. Rosemary Conley's Butternut Squash Soup Recipe

(Ready in about 40 minutes | Serving 2 | Difficulty: Easy)

Per serving: Kcal 195, Fat: 18g, Net Carbs: 27.4g, Protein: 6g

Ingredients:

- 900g (2lb) fresh butternut squash
- 3 celery sticks, sliced
- 2 medium onions, chopped
- 1 garlic clove, crushed
- 2 tsp chopped fresh lemon thyme
- 1 ltr (2pts) vegetable stock
- 2 bay leaves
- Salt and freshly ground black pepper
- 2 tbsp virtually fat-free from age frais
- Chives to garnish

Directions:

1. Using a large cutting knife to cut the squash in half lengthwise. Drop the seeds and, using a small knife, peel the thick skin away. Chop it into little chunks. Place the celery, onions, and garlic in a wide saucepan and fry over low heat for 2-3 mins.

2. Add the thyme, stock, and bay, and gently boil until the vegetables are tender. Remove the bay and, when smooth, liquidize.

3. If possible, return the soup to the tub, change the consistency with a little additional stock, and season with salt and black pepper.

4. Remove from the heat just before serving and whisk in the fried cheese. Divide into bowls for serving.

5. Serve a slice of cheese and a sprinkle of finely chopped chives with the butternut squash broth.

Chapter 4. Herbal Tea Recipes

16. Postpartum Nourish Tea

(Ready in 5 min| serve 4| Difficulty: Normal)

Per serving: Kcal 226.5, Fat: 0.8g, Net Carbs:12.6g, Protein: 13.5g

Ingredients:

- 2 parts gotu kola
- 2 parts lemon balm
- 1-part nettle leaf
- 1-part oat straw
- 1-part milky oat tops
- 1-part chamomile

Directions:

1. Pour 4 cups of hot water over 3 to 4 tablespoons of tea. Steep for 5 to 15 minutes.

17. Respiratory Help

(Ready in about 10 minutes | Serving 1| Difficulty: Easy)

Per serving: Kcal 140, Fat: 8g, Net Carbs: 8g, Protein: 10g

Ingredients:

- 3 parts eucalyptus

- 3 parts fennel seeds

- 3 parts ginger

- 3 parts peppermint

- 2 parts hyssops

- 1-part elecampane root

- 1-part clove

- 0.25-part licorice root

Directions:

1. Pour over 1 tablespoon of tea with 1.5 cups of hot water.

18. Candida Support

(Ready in about 15 minutes | Serving 1| Difficulty: Easy)

Per serving: Kcal 140, Fat: 8g, Net Carbs: 8g, Protein: 10g

Ingredients:

- 5 parts pau D'Arcy
- 2 parts milky oat tops
- 2 parts cedar tips (optional)
- 1-part thyme
- 1-part mint
- 1-part calendula
- 0.5-part oregano
- 0.5-part clove

Directions:

1. Pour over 2 teaspoons of tea with 1.5 cups of hot water.

2. Steep for ten to fifteen minutes.

19. Nursing Mama Tea

(Ready in about 15 minutes | Serving 1| Difficulty: Easy)

Per serving: Kcal 140, Fat: 8g, Net Carbs: 8g, Protein: 10g

Ingredients:

- 10 parts fenugreek seeds
- 5 parts mint
- 5 parts fennels
- 4 parts nettle leaf
- 2 parts lemon balm
- 2 parts goat's rue
- 2 parts alfalfa
- 2 parts chamomiles

Directions:

1. Pour over 3 to 4 teaspoons of tea with 4 cups of hot water.
2. For 5 to 15 minutes, steep.

20. Calm Waters

(Ready in about 15 minutes | Serving 1| Difficulty: Easy)

Per serving: Kcal 140, Fat: 8g, Net Carbs: 8g, Protein: 10g

Ingredients:

- 1-part dried cranberries
- 1-part dried blueberries
- 1-part Oregon grape root
- 1 part of corn silk
- 0.5-part nettle leaf
- 0.5-part ova ursi
- 0.5-part hibiscus
- 0.5-part dandelion leaf

Directions:

1. Pour over 1 tablespoon of tea with 1.5 cups of hot water.

2. Steep in 5-10 minutes.

Chapter 5. Dessert Recipes

21. Carrot Cake

(Ready in 30 min| serve12| Difficulty: Normal)

Per serving: Kcal 226.5, Fat: 0.8g, Net Carbs:12.6g, Protein: 13.5g

Ingredients:

- ¾ cup 100% pure maple syrup

- 1 8-ounce can crush pineapple, drained (about ¾ cup)

- ⅓ cup unsweetened applesauce

- 1 tablespoon ground flaxseeds

- 1⅔ cups spelt flour

- 2¼ teaspoons baking powder

- ¾ teaspoon baking soda

- ½ teaspoon salt

- 1½ teaspoons ground cinnamon

- ½ teaspoon ground nutmeg

- ½ teaspoon ground ginger

- ¼ teaspoon ground allspice

- 3 medium carrots, peeled and grated (about 1½ cups)

- ¾ cup golden raisins

- ½ cup unsweetened shredded coconut

- 1 batch Vanilla Bean Whip, optional

Directions:

1. Preheat the furnace to 350°F.

2. Get an 8 to 8-inch nonstick or silicone baking pan available for you.

3. Whisk together the maple syrup, cracked pineapple, applesauce, and ground flaxseeds vigorously in a large mug. Sift together the spelt flour, baking powder, baking soda, garlic, nutmeg, cinnamon, ginger and allspice.

4. Mix thoroughly. The grated carrots, raisins, and shredded coconut are rolled in. In the prepared tub, pour the batter into it. Bake for 28 to 32 minutes or until it is clean with a toothpick inserted into the middle.

5. Take the cake from the oven and leave for about 30 minutes to cool in the pan. Until frosting with Vanilla Bean Whip or serving alone, put the cake on a cooling rack and cool completely.

22. Double Chocolate Cupcakes

(Ready in 30 min| serve12| Difficulty: Normal)

Per serving: Kcal 226.5, Fat: 0.8g, Net Carbs:12.6g, Protein: 13.5g

Ingredients:

- 2 ounces unsweetened chocolate

- 1 cup unsweetened plant-based milk

- 1 teaspoon apple cider vinegar

- ⅔ cup dry sweetener

- ¼ cup unsweetened applesauce

- 1 teaspoon pure vanilla extract

- 1 cup whole-wheat pastry flour, or spelt flour

- ⅓ cup cocoa powder, either Dutch-processed or regular unsweetened

- ¾ teaspoon baking soda

- ½ teaspoon baking powder

- ¼ teaspoon salt

- 1 batch Fudgy Chocolate Frosting

Directions:

1. Preheat the furnace to 350°F. Line a muffin pan with silicone liners for 12 cups or have a nonstick or silicone muffin pan available.

2. In the oven, melt the chocolate in a little cup. Only put aside. Whisk the plant-based milk and vinegar together in a large tub. Let it sit until it curdles for a few minutes.

3. Add the dry sweetener, applesauce, vanilla and melted chocolate and mix well. Sift the flour, cocoa powder, baking soda, baking powder and salt together in a separate dish.

4. Apply the paste, one half at a time, to the wet ingredients and beat until no major lumps remain.

5. Scoop the batter into the prepared tub, filling three-quarters for each cup.

6. Bake for 18 to 20 minutes or until it is clean with a toothpick inserted into the middle.

7. Remove the cupcakes from the oven and allow the cupcakes to cool for at least 20 minutes, then carefully place a knife around each cupcake's edges to remove them.

8. Before frosting with the Fudgy Chocolate Frosting, the cupcakes should be perfectly cool.

23. Fudgy Chocolate Frosting

(Ready in 30 min| serve1| Difficulty: Normal)

Per serving: Kcal 226.5, Fat: 0.8g, Net Carbs:12.6g, Protein: 13.5g

Ingredients:

- 1 cup boiling water

- ⅓ cup unsweetened cocoa powder

- 1½ cups dried, pitted dates, tough ends removed

- 1 tablespoon brown rice syrup

- Pinch salt

- ½ teaspoon pure vanilla extract

Directions:

1. In a mixer, place the hot water and cocoa powder.

2. Blend for about 30 seconds at high rpm, or until the mixture is fairly smooth. Scrape the blender's sides off. Be cautious not to encourage the buildup of steam.

3. Add to the blender the dates, brown rice syrup, and salt. Blend until smooth, sometimes stopping to scrape with a spatula down the sides of the blender to ensure that all ingredients are integrated.

4. Add vanilla and combine until mixed together. Shift the mixture to a tub that is airtight. Let it chill completely, until it becomes solid and spreadable, for at least 3 hours.

24. Ginger Peach Muffins

(Ready in 30 min| serve14| Difficulty: Normal)

Per serving: Kcal 226.5, Fat: 0.8g, Net Carbs:12.6g, Protein: 13.5g

Ingredients:

- 1 cup unsweetened plant-based milk

- 1 tablespoon ground flaxseeds

- 1 teaspoon apple cider vinegar

- 2¼ cups spelt flour

- ¾ cup dry sweetener

- 1 tablespoon baking powder

- ½ teaspoon salt

- 2 teaspoons ground ginger

- 1 teaspoon ground cinnamon

- ¾ cup unsweetened applesauce

- 1 teaspoon pure vanilla extract

- 4 medium peaches, peeled, halved, pitted, and cut into ¼-inch slices (about 2 cups)

Directions:

1. Preheat the furnace to 350°F. Line a muffin pan with silicone liners for 12 cups or have a nonstick or silicone muffin pan available.

2. Using a fork to aggressively mix together the plant-based milk, flaxseeds, and vinegar in a large measuring cup.

3. Combine for about a minute, or before foamy emerges. Only put aside. Sift together the flour, dried sweetener, baking powder, salt, ginger, and cinnamon in a medium mixing cup.

4. In the middle of the mixture, make a well and pour in the mixture of milk.

5. Add the vanilla and then applesauce, and stir together in the well with the milk mixture.

6. Only after the dry ingredients are integrated into the wet ingredients, add the dry ingredients (do not overmix).

7. Fold the peaches in. All the way to the top, fill each muffin cup. Bake for 24 to 27 minutes.

8. Until it comes out clean with a knife inserted into the middle. Remove the pan from the oven. Let the muffins absolutely cool off, about 20 minutes. Run a knife gently around the sides of each muffin for a few minutes to cut it.

25. Oat berry Yogurt Muffins

(Ready in 30 min| serve1| Difficulty: Normal)

Per serving: Kcal 226.5, Fat: 0.8g, Net Carbs:12.6g, Protein: 13.5g

Ingredients:

- 2¼ cups oat flour

- 1 tablespoon baking powder

- ¾ teaspoon salt

- ½ cup dry sweetener

- ⅔ cup unsweetened plant-based milk

- ½ cup unsweetened applesauce

- ½ cup unsweetened plain soy yogurt

- 2 teaspoons pure vanilla extract

- 1¼ cup berries (such as blueberries, raspberries, or blackberries), halved

Directions:

1. Preheat the furnace to 350°F. Line up a 12-cup muffin tray with liners of silicone or Have a non-stick or silicone muffin pan packed.

2. Sift together the flour, baking powder, salt, and dry sweetener in a medium mixing cup.

3. In the middle, make a well and pour in the milk, applesauce, yogurt, and vanilla, depending on the vine. In the well, stir the wet ingredients together.

4. Then add the wet and dry ingredients before the dry ingredients are humidified (do not overmix).

5. Fold the berries in. 3/4 of the way, fill each muffin cup and bake for 22 to 26 minutes. It should come out clean with a knife inserted through the middle.

6. Let the muffins cool completely for about 20 minutes, then carefully loop a knife along each muffin's edges to cut it.

Chapter 6. Snacks and Sides Recipes

26. Rosemary Endives

Ready in about 30 minutes | Serving 2-4 | Difficulty: Normal)

Per serving: Kcal 134, Fat: 4g, Net Carbs: 6g, Protein: 4g

Ingredients:

- 2 tbsps. Olive oil

- 1 tsp. dried rosemary

- 2 halved endives

- ¼ tsp. black pepper

- ½ tsp. turmeric powder

Directions:

1. In a baking pan, combine the endives with the oil and the other ingredients, toss gently, introduce in the oven and bake at 400 0F for 20 minutes. Divide between plates and serve.

27. Fiesta Corn Bread

(Ready in about 45 minutes | Serving 9 | Difficulty: Normal)

Per serving: Kcal 140, Fat: 8g, Net Carbs: 8g, Protein: 10g

Ingredients:

- 1 cup cornmeal

- 1 cup whole wheat pastry flour

- 1 teaspoon baking powder

- 1 teaspoon baking soda

- ½ teaspoon of sea salt

- ½ teaspoon tarragon

- ¾ cup corn, fresh off the cob or thawed

- 1/3 cup unsweetened applesauce

- 2 tablespoons maple syrup

- 1 egg replacer (1 tablespoon ground flaxseed meal with 3 tablespoons water)

- 1 1/3 cups soy milk

Directions:

1. Preheat the oven to 350 degrees.

2. In a big bowl, add the cornmeal, flour, baking powder, baking soda, salt, and tarragon and mix well.

3. Connect the dry ingredients to the corn, applesauce, and maple syrup, and blend. Add egg substitute and milk, and stir until all is well combined.

4. Pour into a baking dish that is 9 to 9 nonstick.

5. Bake for 35 minutes or until the top is firm and a knife is cleanly inserted into the middle.

28. Raisin Walnut Bread

(Ready in about 60 minutes | Serving 2 | Difficulty: Normal)

Per serving: Kcal 140, Fat: 8g, Net Carbs: 8g, Protein: 10g

Ingredients:

- 2 cups whole wheat pastry flour
- 1 teaspoon baking powder
- 1 teaspoon baking soda
- ¼ cup maple syrup
- 1 cup nondairy milk
- 1 small banana, mashed
- 1 cup raisins
- ½ cup walnuts

Directions:

1. Preheat the oven to 350 degrees.

2. In a large mixing bowl, combine the flour, baking powder, and baking soda together. Stir in the syrup, honey, banana, walnuts, and raisins. Stir to blend just enough. The batter will be very rigid and sticky.

3. Spoon and bake for 45 minutes in a nonstick loaf pan. Remove the pan from the oven and set it to cool on a rack.

29. Sensational Herb Bread

(Ready in about 1 hr. 40 minutes | Serving 2 | Difficulty: Normal)

Per serving: Kcal 140, Fat: 8g, Net Carbs: 8g, Protein: 10g

Ingredients:

- 2 1/3 cups whole wheat pastry flour
- ½ tablespoon rosemary
- ½ tablespoon oregano
- 1 teaspoon thyme
- 1 teaspoon basil
- 1 tablespoon onion powder
- ½ teaspoon of sea salt
- 2 teaspoons instant (fast rise) yeast
- 2 teaspoons molasses
- 1 cup lukewarm water

Directions:

1. In a large mixing bowl, combine the flour, spices, and salt. Stir the yeast in.

2. Create a well in the flour center and pour the molasses and water in. To make a smooth, slightly wet dough, mix by hand. Knead until the dough leaves the bowl's sides clean and appears elastic.

3. In a nonstick (small) bread pan, place the dough, cover with oiled plastic wrap, and leave to double for about 1 hour in a warm, draft-free place.

4. Preheat the oven for around 35 minutes to 350 ° F.5 | Bake. Test it by tapping the top with your knuckles to see if the bread is ready. Bread, when it sounds hollow, is over.

30. Quick no fat Cranberry Bread

(Ready in about 60 minutes | Serving 2 | Difficulty: Normal)

Per serving: Kcal 140, Fat: 8g, Net Carbs: 8g, Protein: 10g

Ingredients:

- 2 cups whole wheat pastry flour

- ¾ cup Sucanat

- 1 teaspoon baking powder

- 1 teaspoon baking soda

- 1 cup of orange juice

- 1 egg replacer (1 tablespoon ground flaxseed meal with 3 tablespoons water)

- 1½ cups fresh cranberries, finely chopped in food processor

- ½ cup chopped walnuts

Directions:

1. Preheat the oven to 350 degrees.

2. Mix together a big bowl of flour, Sucanat, baking powder, and baking soda.

3. Stir in the egg replacer and orange juice. Mix until thoroughly combined.

4. Fold in the nuts and cranberries. Spread in a nonstick bread pan evenly.

5. Bake for about 45 minutes or until the toothpick inserted in the center is clean. Until removing it from the pan, cool for 15 minutes.

31. Quick Apple Loaf

(Ready in about 45 minutes | Serving 2 | Difficulty: Normal)

Per serving: Kcal 140, Fat: 8g, Net Carbs: 8g, Protein: 10g

Ingredients:

- 2 cups whole wheat pastry flour

- ½ cup Sucanat

- 1 teaspoon cinnamon

- ½ teaspoon baking soda

- 1 teaspoon baking powder

- ½ teaspoon nutmeg

- ½ teaspoon ginger

- ¼ teaspoon salt

- 1 ripe banana, mashed

- 1 cup nondairy milk

- 1 teaspoon vanilla extract

- ½ cup chopped walnuts

- 1 cup apples, peeled and diced

Directions:

1. Preheat the oven to 350 degrees.

2. In a mixing bowl, add flour, sucanat, cinnamon, baking soda, baking powder, nutmeg, ginger, and salt.

3. Mash the banana in a different, larger bowl and stir in the non-dairy milk and vanilla. Thoroughly blend. Apply the flour mixture, apples, and walnuts.

4. Spread in 9 to 9 nonstick baking pan and bake until a toothpick inserted into the middle comes out clean for 30 to 35 minutes.

32. Breakfast Home fry Hash

(Ready in about 35 minutes | Serving 4 | Difficulty: Normal)

Per serving: Kcal 140, Fat: 8g, Net Carbs: 8g, Protein: 10g

Ingredients:

- 4 large potatoes, scrubbed and sliced
- 6 tablespoons vegetable broth, divided
- 1 onion, thinly sliced
- 1 green bell pepper, diced
- 4 teaspoons light soy sauce or tamari
- ¼ teaspoon black pepper
- 6 cherry tomatoes, cut into quarters
- 2 green onions, thinly sliced

Directions:

1. Cut the potatoes into ½-inch cubes and steam them until just tender when pierced with a sharp knife, about 10 minutes. Remove from heat and set aside.

2. Heat 3 tablespoons of vegetable broth in a large nonstick skillet over medium-high heat, and add the onion and green pepper. Cook, stirring frequently.

3. Add the diced potatoes, 3 tablespoons vegetable broth, soy sauce or tamari, and black pepper. Cook, turning gently with a spatula until the potatoes are golden brown.

4. Garnish with cherry tomatoes and green onions.

33. Favorite French Toast

(Ready in about 30 minutes | Serving 8 | Difficulty: Normal)

Per serving: Kcal 140, Fat: 8g, Net Carbs: 8g, Protein: 10g

Ingredients:

- 1 cup vanilla soy (or almond) milk

- 1 tablespoon Sucanat

- 2 tablespoons flaxseed meal (do not mix with water)

- 1½ teaspoons pumpkin pie spice

- 1 teaspoon vanilla extract

- 8 slices whole-grain bread fresh fruit and syrup, for topping

Directions:

1. In a large mixing bowl, blend milk, Sucanat, egg replacer powder, pumpkin pie spice, and vanilla extract to shape the batter.

2. Dip one side of the bread quickly into the batter and repeat with the other side.

3. Over medium-high heat, fry in a nonstick skillet until golden brown.

4. Using fresh fruit, fruit preserves, or syrup to serve.

34. Fruit Crepes

(Ready in about 30 minutes | Serving 6| Difficulty: Normal)

Per serving: Kcal 140, Fat: 8g, Net Carbs: 8g, Protein: 10g

Ingredients:

For the crepes

- 1 cup whole wheat pastry flour

- 2 egg replacers (2 tablespoons ground flaxseed meal with 6 tablespoons water)

- 1½ cups nondairy milk

For the fruit filling

- 1/3 cup strawberries, sliced

- 1/3 cup blueberries

- 1/3 cup peaches, sliced

- 1/8 cup walnuts, finely chopped

- 1 teaspoon cinnamon

- 4 tablespoons maple syrup

Directions:

1. Place the flour in a medium bowl to create the crepes. Combine the egg and milk substitutes and apply to the flour mixture. Beat until the batter is smooth, using a wire whisk. Batters ought to be thin. When required, add more milk.

2. Over medium heat, heat a nonstick skillet until hot. Distribute the batter uniformly over the bottom of the pan using a 1/4 cup scale. Tilt and rotate the pan until the batter is uniformly dispersed. Cook the crepe on the bottom until it is cooked. Flip the crepe and cook, on the other hand, briefly. Withdraw to a flat plate. With the remaining batter, repeat this operation.

3. Thin it with a little extra milk if the batter thickens when producing the crepes.

4. In a saucepan, mix cinnamon, Sucanat, and fruit over low heat for fruit filling. Stir continuously until sugar and fruit are mixed, and the fruit is lightly cooked. Mix the ingredients.

5. Place 1–2 tablespoons of fruit mixture on one side of the crepe, taking 1 crepe at a time. Over the fruit mixture, fold the other side of the crepe. Drizzle and sprinkle with maple syrup and cinnamon. Garnish with fresh fruit.

35. G Moms Oatmeal

(Ready in about 10 minutes | Serving 3| Difficulty: Normal)

Per serving: Kcal 140, Fat: 8g, Net Carbs: 8g, Protein: 10g

Ingredients:

- 2 cups of water
- 1 cup "old fashioned" oats
- ½ cup raisins
- ½ cup blueberries
- 2 teaspoons maple syrup, divided
- ½ cup sliced strawberries
- 1–2 kiwis, peeled and diced
- Cinnamon to taste
- Flaxseed
- Walnuts, chopped (optional)

Directions:

1. Boil water, add oats and raisins, and (2-3 minutes) stir until thick.

2. Place the blueberries in a serving bowl at the bottom. Drizzle with 1 teaspoon of maple syrup.

3. Pour a mixture of cooked oatmeal over the blueberries. Lay strawberries on top of the oatmeal and kiwi. Sprinkle with cinnamon and flaxseed generously, drizzle with 1 teaspoon of maple syrup, and add chopped walnuts.

Chapter 7. Grains and Main Dishes

36. Italian-Style Stuffed Tomatoes

(Ready in 20min| serve4| Difficulty: Normal)

Per serving: Kcal 152.3, Fat: 8.4g, Net Carbs: 3.7g, Protein: 5.6g

Ingredients:

- 4 cups cooked navy beans, or two 15-ounce cans, drained and rinsed

- One 15-ounce can artichoke hearts (oil-free), drained and roughly chopped

- ½ medium yellow onion, peeled and diced small

- ½ cup Basil Pesto

- 6 large tomatoes, such as beefsteak

Directions:

1. In a small bowl, combine the beans, the artichoke heart, the onion, and the pesto and set aside.

2. Cut each tomato's top ½ inch off and scoop the flesh out, leaving a ½-inch shell.

3. Divide the filling evenly between the tomatoes prepared and arrange them for serving on a platter or between individual plates.

37. Brown Basmati Rice Pilaf

(Ready in about 40 minutes | Serving 2-4 | Difficulty: Normal)

Per serving: Kcal 263, Fat: 17g, Net Carbs: 40.4g, Protein: 13g

Ingredients:

- ½ tbsp. vegan butter
- ½ c. mushrooms, chopped
- ½ c. brown basmati rice
- 3 tbsps. water
- 1/8 tsp. dried thyme
- Ground pepper to taste
- ½ tbsp. olive oil
- ¼ c. green onion, chopped
- 1 c. vegetable broth
- ¼ tsp. salt
- ¼ c. chopped, toasted pecans

Directions:

1. Over medium-low pressure, position a saucepan. Add the oil and butter.

2. When it melts, mushrooms are added and cook until tender.

3. Stir in the brown rice and the green onion. For 3 minutes, cook. Revolve endlessly.

4. Incorporate the soup, sugar, salt and thyme.

5. Lower the heat and cover it with a cap as it starts to bubble. Simmer until it is prepared with rice. If ordered, add more water or broth.

6. Add the pecans and vinegar, stirring.

7. Serve.

38. Thai Red Curry

(Ready in about 40 minutes | Serving 2-4 | Difficulty: Normal)

Per serving: Kcal 251, Fat: 10g, Net Carbs: 40.4g, Protein: 13g

Ingredients:

- 1 ½ c. packed thinly sliced kale

- Pinch of salt to taste

- 2 tbsps. Thai red curry paste

- 1 tbsp. soy sauce

- 1 ¼ c. long-grain brown jasmine rice

- 1 small white onion, chopped

- 1 tbsp. grated ginger

- 1 red bell pepper

- 1 tbsp. coconut oil or olive oil

- ½ c. water

- 1 ½ tsps. coconut sugar or turbinado sugar

- 2 cloves garlic

- 2 tsps. lime juice

- 3 carrots, peeled and sliced

- 1 bell pepper

- 1 can (14 oz.) regular coconut milk

Instructions:

1. Bring a big pot of water and bring it to a boil to make rice. To avoid excess, insert the rinsed rice and begin to boil for 30 minutes, reducing heat when necessary. Drain the rice, remove it from the heat, and place the rice back in the tank. Cover and let the rice sit for 10 minutes or longer until you are ready to eat. Just before eating, season the rice with salt and fluff it with a fork to taste.

2. Fire up a large skillet over the medium fire with the deep sides to make the curry, then add your oil until warm. Then add the onion and a sprinkle of salt and simmer until the onion has softened and becomes translucent, continually stirring for about 5 minutes. Garlic and ginger are introduced and cook for around 25-30 seconds while continually stirring until fragrant.

3. Attach the carrots and your bell peppers, roast, occasionally stirring, 3 to 5 minutes more, until these bell peppers are fork-tender. Then add your

curry paste and simmer, constantly stirring, for around 2 minutes.

4. To blend, add water, kale, coconut milk and sugar and whisk. Bring the mixture to a boil over a medium flame. To maintain a moderate simmer, reduce the flame as required and cook until the carrots, peppers, and kale have softened to your taste, stirring for around 5-10 minutes periodically.

5. Take the pot from the blaze and season with tamari and rice vinegar. To taste, add salt (for the best flavor). If a little more energy is needed for your curry, add 1⁄2 teaspoon more tamari, or add 1⁄2 teaspoon more rice vinegar for more acidity. Divide the curry and rice into bowls and garnish with sliced cilantro and a splash of red pepper flakes, if you prefer. Serve on the side if you prefer hot curries, with sriracha or chili garlic sauce.

6. If you want to add tofu, first bake it and add coconut milk to it. It would eat up too much of the fat if you add raw tofu, so baking it will considerably increase the taste, anyway.

39. Lovage and Lemon Roasted Chicken

(Ready in about 40 minutes | Serving 2-4 | Difficulty: Normal)

Per serving: Kcal 251, Fat: 10g, Net Carbs: 40.4g, Protein: 13g

Ingredients:

- 1 handful lovage leaves and stems

- 1 lemon sliced

- 4 chicken legs whole, bone in 1 onion chopped several carrots and/or potatoes, chopped

- sea salt to taste pepper to taste

Directions:

1. Preheat the oven to 350 degrees Celsius. In the bottom of a large baking sheet lie a bed of lovage.

2. Tuck a lemon slice under the skin of the chicken legs, and enjoy the leaves. In the pan, position the thighs. Sprinkle with pepper and salt and drizzle with olive oil. Throw the chicken about with some chopped onion and carrots. Bake for 30 minutes, sealed, uncovered for a further 30 minutes, or until the chicken skin is crisp.

40. Garlic Bacon Kale

(Ready in about 40 minutes | Serving 2-4 | Difficulty: Normal)

Per serving: Kcal 231, Fat: 12g, Net Carbs: 30.4g, Protein: 10g

Ingredients:

- 3 slices bacon chopped
- ½ cup onion finely chopped
- 1 bunch kale washed
- 2 cloves garlic minced salt & pepper to taste

Directions:

1. Over medium pressure, fry the bacon until crisp. Remove the bacon and reserve the drippings. Reduce the heat to medium-low and cook the onion until tender, about 10 minutes, in the drippings.

2. Attach the kale and garlic and stir until done, 5 minutes or so. To taste, season with salt and pepper. Sprinkle and serve with bacon.

41. Spicy Kale and Coconut Fried Rice

(Ready in about 40 minutes | Serving 2-4 | Difficulty: Normal)

Per serving: Kcal 231, Fat: 10g, Net Carbs: 36g, Protein: 7g

Ingredients:

- 2 tablespoons coconut oil or quality high-heat oil such as avocado oil, divided

- 2 eggs, whisked together with a dash of salt

- 2 big cloves garlic, pressed or minced

- ¾ cup chopped green onions (about 1 bunch)

- Optional: 1 cup chopped vegetables, like bell pepper, carrot or Brussels sprouts

- 1 medium bunch kale (preferably Lacinato but curly green is good, too), ribs removed and leaves chopped

- ¼ teaspoon fine sea salt

- ¾ cup large, unsweetened coconut flakes* (not shredded coconut)

- 2 cups cooked and chilled brown rice**

- 2 teaspoons reduced-sodium tamari or soy sauce

- 2 teaspoons chili garlic sauce or sriracha

- 1 lime, halved Handful fresh cilantro, for garnish.

Instructions:

1. On medium-high fire, heat a big (12-inch or broader) wok, cast-iron skillet or nonstick frying pan. Add 1-teaspoon of oil and rotate the pan to cover the bottom until the pan is hot enough for a drop of water to sizzle on touch.

2. Pour in the eggs and simmer until the eggs are scrambled and lightly set, stirring regularly. To your clean cup, pass the eggs. Wipe the pan with a paper towel if necessary (be careful, it's hot!).

3. In a skillet, add 1-tablespoon of oil and add garlic, green onions and optional extra vegetables to the pan. Cook for 30 seconds or longer until fragrant or until the vegetables are soft, stirring regularly. The kale and salt are applied.

4. Continue to cook until the kale, stirring regularly, is wilted and crispy, about 1 to 2 minutes. Move the contents of your pan to your egg tray. To the pan, add the remaining 2-teaspoons of oil. Pour in the coconut flakes and cook for about 30 seconds, continually stirring, until the flakes are softly golden.

5. Add the rice to the pan and cook, stirring regularly, for about 3 minutes, until the rice is sweet. Pour the bowl's contents back into the bowl, and the spatula or spoon will break up the scrambled egg. Remove the pan from the heat once warmed.

6. Put in the tamari, chili garlic sauce and 1⁄2 lime juice. Stir to mix. Taste, and add another teaspoon of tamari or a pinch of salt if it's not fantastic yet as needed. Slice the remaining 1⁄2 lime into wedges, then divide into individual bowls with the fried rice. For anyone who may like more, garnish with wedges of lime and a sprinkling of broken cilantro leaves and jars of tamari, chili garlic sauce and red pepper flakes on the hand.

42. Garlicky Mushrooms and Kale

(Ready in about 40 minutes | Serving 2-4 | Difficulty: Normal)

Per serving: Kcal 231, Fat: 10g, Net Carbs: 36g, Protein: 7g

Ingredients:

- 1 teaspoon olive oil

- 6 cloves garlic, minced

- 1/4 teaspoon salt

- 8 ounces cremini or button mushrooms, sliced (about 2 cups)

- 1 pound kale, coarse stems removed, leaves sliced or torn into pieces

- Several pinches of freshly ground black pepper

Directions:

1. Over medium heat, preheat a large skillet. Sauté the garlic for about 2 minutes in the oil, taking care not to smoke it. If required, spray it with a bit of nonstick cooking spray. Sprinkle on the salt and

add the mushrooms. Let them cook for 5 to 7 minutes, stirring regularly, until the mushrooms are lightly browned and the moisture is released.

2. Attach the kale and pepper, and sauté for about 10-more minutes with the tongs. If the pan appears empty, apply splashes of water. The kale should be tender and fairly well baked. Immediately serve.

43. Char-Grilled Beef with a Red Wine Jus, Onion Rings, Garlic Kale, and Herb-Roasted Potatoes

(Ready in about 40 minutes | Serving 2-4 | Difficulty: Normal)

Per serving: Kcal 291, Fat: 20g, Net Carbs: 46g, Protein: 17g

Ingredients:

- 1 / 2 cup (100g) potatoes, peeled and cut into 3 / 4 -inch (2cm) diced pieces

- 1 tablespoon extra-virgin olive oil

- 2 tablespoons (5g) parsley, finely chopped

- 1 / 3 cup (50g) red onion, sliced into rings

- 2 ounces (50g) kale, sliced

- 2 garlic cloves, finely chopped

- 1 x 4- to 5-ounce (120 to 150g) beef tenderloin (about 1 1 / 2 inch or 3.5cm thick) or sirloin steak (3 / 4 inch or 2cm thick)

- 3 tablespoons (40ml) red wine

- 5 / 8 cup (150ml) beef stock

- 1 teaspoon tomato purée

- 1 teaspoon corn flour, dissolved in

- 1 tablespoon water

Directions:

1. Heat the oven to 220oC (425oF). Place the potatoes in a boiling water saucepan, bring to a boil again and simmer for 4 to 5 minutes, then drain. Put 1-teaspoon of oil in the roasting pan and roast for 35 to 45 minutes in the hot oven. Switch the potatoes and make sure they cook evenly after 10 minutes.

2. Remove from the oven until baked, sprinkle with chopped parsley, and blend properly. Over medium heat, fry the onion in 1 teaspoon of oil for 5 to 7 minutes, until soft and nicely caramelized. Just stay wet. For 2 to 3 minutes, steam the kale, then rinse. Gently fry the garlic in 1/2 teaspoon of oil, until soft but not browned, for 1 minute. Attach the kale and fry for an extra 1 to 2 minutes, until tender. Just stay wet.

3. Over high pressure, heat an ovenproof frying pan before you smoke. Coat the meat in 1/2 teaspoon of the oil and fry it over medium-high heat in the hot pan as you want the meat done (see our cooking time guide). It would be easier to sear it and then move the pan to an oven set at 4250F (2200C) if you prefer the meat medium and finish the cooking that way for the specified times.

4. Set aside to rest and remove the meat from the pan. To put in some meat residue, add the wine to the hot pan. Simmer to decrease the wine by half until the wine is syrupy and tastes concentrated. In the steak pan, add the stock and tomato purée and bring to a boil, then add the paste of corn-flour to thicken the sauce, adding it a little at a time until you get the consistency you like.

5. Stir in any of the juices from the rested steak, and serve with the roasted potatoes, kale, onion rings, and red wine sauce.

44. Kidney Bean Mole with Baked Potato

(Ready in about 40 minutes | Serving 2-4 | Difficulty: Normal)

Per serving: Kcal 266, Fat: 12g, Net Carbs: 36g, Protein: 9g

Ingredients:

- 1 / 4 cup (40g) red onion, finely chopped

- 1 teaspoon finely chopped fresh ginger

- 2 garlic cloves, finely chopped

- 1 Thai chili, finely chopped

- 1 teaspoon extra-virgin olive oil

- 1 teaspoon ground turmeric

- 1 teaspoon ground cumin pinch of ground clove pinch of ground cinnamon

- 1 medium baking potato

- 7 / 8 cup (190g) canned chopped tomatoes

- 1 teaspoon brown sugar

- 1 / 3 cup (50g) red bell pepper, cored, seeds removed and roughly chopped

- 5 / 8 cup (150ml) vegetable stock

- 1 tablespoon cocoa powder

- 1 teaspoon sesame seeds

- 2 teaspoons peanut butter (smooth if available, but chunky is fine)

- 7 / 8 cup (150) canned kidney beans

- 2 tablespoons (5g) parsley, chopped

Directions:

1. Heat the oven to 200oC (400°F). In a medium saucepan over medium heat, fry the onion, ginger, garlic, and chili in the oil for about 10 minutes until tender. Attach the seasoning, then simmer for 1 to 2 more minutes.

2. Place the potato in the hot oven on a baking tray and bake for 45 to 60 minutes, until the middle is soft (or longer, depending on how crispy the outside maybe).

3. Meanwhile, add to the saucepan the tomatoes, cinnamon, red pepper, stock, cocoa powder, sesame seeds, peanut butter, and kidney beans and gently simmer for 45 to 60 minutes. To end, sprinkle with the parsley.

4. Break the potato in half and serve on top with the mole.

45. Chicken and Kale Curry with Bombay Potatoes

(Ready in about 30 minutes | Serving 2-4 | Difficulty: Normal)

Per serving: Kcal 225, Fat: 17g, Net Carbs: 17.4g, Protein: 8g

Ingredients:

- 4 x 4 1 / 2 - to 5 1 / 2 -ounce (120 to 150g) skinless, boneless chicken breasts, cut into bite-size pieces
- 4 tablespoons extra-virgin olive oil
- 3 tablespoons ground turmeric
- 2 red onions, sliced
- 2 Thai chilies, finely chopped
- 3 garlic cloves, finely chopped
- 1 tablespoon finely chopped fresh ginger
- 1 tablespoon mild curry powder
- 1 x 14-ounce (400g) can chopped tomatoes
- 2 1/8 cups (500ml) chicken stock
- 7/8 cup (200ml) coconut milk

- 2 cardamom pods

- 1 cinnamon stick

- 1 1/3 pounds (600g) russet potatoes

- 1/4 cup (10g) parsley, chopped

- 2 2/3 cups (175g) kale, chopped

- 2 tablespoons (5g) coriander, chopped

Instructions:

1. Rub 1-teaspoon of oil and 1-tablespoon of turmeric with the chicken meat. Keep for 30 minutes to marinate.

2. Fry the chicken over high heat for 4 to 5 minutes until nicely browned and cooked through, then remove from the pan and set aside (there should be enough oil in the marinade to cook the chicken).

3. In a moderate frying pan, heat 1-tablespoon of the oil and add the onion, chili, garlic and ginger. Add the curry powder and another tablespoon of turmeric and cook for another 1 to 2 minutes. Fry

for about 10 minutes, or until tender. Return the tomatoes to the pan and simmer for 2-more minutes. Connect a stick of stock, coconut milk, cinnamon, and cardamom and simmer for 45 to 60 minutes. To ensure that it does not run out, check the pan at frequent intervals, and you will have to add more storage.

4. preheat oven to 220°C (425°F). Peel the potatoes as the curry is simmering and cut them into small chunks. With the left tablespoon of turmeric, put in boiling water and boil for 5 minutes.

5. Drain well and allow for 10 minutes to steam dry. They need to be white around the edges and flaky. Place in the roasting pan, toss with the remaining oil and roast for 30 minutes or until brown and crisp.

6. When they're set, toss through the parsley. Add the kale, cooked chicken, and coriander when the curry has the necessary consistency and cook for another 5 minutes to ensure that the chicken is cooked through and then served with the potatoes.

46. Turkey Mole Tacos

(Ready in about 30 minutes | Serving 2-4 | Difficulty: Normal)

Per serving: Kcal 225, Fat: 17g, Net Carbs: 17.4g, Protein: 8g

Ingredients:

- 75 pound Lean ground turkey

- 4 stalks Green onion, chopped

- 2 Garlic cloves, minced

- 1 rib Celery, chopped

- 3.5 ounces Roasted sweet peppers, chopped and drained

- 7 ounces Diced tomatoes, canned

- 6 Corn tortillas, 6 inches, warmed

- 1 Red onion, thinly sliced

- 2 tablespoons Walnuts, roasted, chopped

- 2 ounces Dark chocolate, chopped

- .25 teaspoon Sea salt

- 4 teaspoons Chili powder

- 5 teaspoon Cumin

- .125 teaspoon Cinnamon, ground

Directions:

1. Cook the ground turkey with green onions, celery and garlic in a large non-stick skillet over medium heat. The turkey has hit a temperature of one hundred and sixty-five degrees, and the vegetables are juicy. Cook until no pink remains.

2. Connect the dried tomatoes, roasted red peppers, sugar, cocoa, chili powder, cumin, and sea salt to a pan with the fried turkey. The heat to medium-low, cause the liquid from the tomatoes to boil, cover the skillet with a lid and simmer for ten minutes. To avoid sticking and fire, stir regularly.

3. Stir in the walnuts and extract the cooked ground turkey from the heat.

4. Divide the taco meat with the sliced red onion between the corn tortillas, topping it off. When wet, serve.

47. Sweet and Sour Tofu

(Ready in about 20 minutes | Serving 2-4 | Difficulty: Normal)

Per serving: Kcal 175, Fat: 14g, Net Carbs: 10g, Protein: 17g

Ingredients:

- 14 ounces Tofu, firm
- 8 tablespoons Corn-starch, divided
- 1 Egg white
- 1 cup Pineapple, chopped
- 2 Bell pepper, chopped
- 6 tablespoons Rice vinegar
- 6 tablespoons Date sugar
- 2 tablespoons Tamari sauce
- 1 teaspoon Sea salt
- 2 tablespoons Tomato paste
- 2 teaspoons Water
- 2 tablespoons Corn-starch
- 1 teaspoon Sesame seeds, toasted

Directions:

1. Strip a baking sheet of aluminum with kitchen parchment or a sheet of silicone and set the oven to three hundred- and fifty-degrees Fahrenheit.

2. Start by pressing the tofu and then slicing it into bite-sized cubes. Sprinkle over the tofu with two of the eight broken teaspoons of corn-starch, tossing it before the tofu is uniformly covered.

3. Put in one bowl the remaining six tablespoons of divided corn-starch and in another the egg white (or aquafaba).

4. At a time, dip a few cubes of tofu first in the white egg and then in the corn-starch. To the prepared baking sheet, move the breaded cubes and resume the process until all the cubes are prepared. Arrange the tofu cubes equally in the pan to don't hit, then bake for around fifteen to twenty minutes until crisp.

5. Combine the rice vinegar, date syrup, tamari sauce, sea salt, tomato paste, water, two tablespoons of corn starch, and sesame seeds while the tofu is frying.

6. In a large pan, add the peppers and pineapple and saute them until slightly tender. Apply the blended sauce to the pan and deglaze it. Add the fried tofu to the skillet and finish frying it in the sauce until it is covered and moist and the sauce thickens.

7. Serve over brown rice or buckwheat when it is warm.

48. BBQ Tempeh Sandwiches

(Ready in about 40 minutes | Serving 2-4 | Difficulty: Normal)

Per serving: Kcal 225, Fat: 24g, Net Carbs: 20g, Protein: 17g

Ingredients:

- 8 ounces Tempeh, sliced into long strips
- .75 cup Barbecue sauce
- .5 teaspoon Liquid smoke
- 1.5 cups Red cabbage, shredded
- .5 cup Carrots, shredded
- .5 cup Red onion, diced
- .5 teaspoon Date sugar
- 1.5 teaspoons Sea salt
- 1 tablespoon Apple cider vinegar
- .5 teaspoon Garlic powder
- 2 tablespoons Mayonnaise
- .25 teaspoon Black pepper, ground
- 4 Whole wheat buns

Directions:

1. Put the sliced tempeh and wrap it in the barbecue sauce and the liquid smoke in a glass baking dish. Although the liquid smoke doesn't have to be added, it's a nice touch that helps it taste as though it had rolled off the grill freshly. Give at least forty-five minutes for the dish to marinate.

2. When the tempeh is almost done, start marinating to preheat your oven to four hundred-and fifty-degrees Fahrenheit.

3. Cover the tempeh in an aluminum sheet, let it steam for the first 30 minutes, then cut the aluminum and cook for an extra five minutes.

4. In the meantime, by mixing the remaining ingredients (except for the buns) in a dish, prepare the slaw. Cover the bowl until mixed and allow it to melt in the refrigerator until the tempeh is baked. When you first put the tempeh in the oven, it is better to make the slaw, rather than at the end, as it takes the flavors longer to meld.

5. Break the buns' tempeh strips to serve and then top them off with the slaw.

49. Tofu Tikka Masala

(Ready in about 35 minutes | Serving: 4 | Difficulty: Normal)

Ingredients:

- 14 ounces Tofu, extra-firm, sliced into bite-sized cubes

- 1 teaspoon Cumin

- 2 teaspoons Ginger, peeled and grated

- .5 teaspoon Sweet paprika

- .5 teaspoon Turmeric

- 2 cloves Garlic, minced

- 1.5 teaspoons Garam masala

- .5 teaspoon Coriander powder

- .25 teaspoon Cayenne

- 1 cup Tomato passata (if not available, use puree)

- 14 ounces Coconut milk, full-fat

- 2 tablespoons Olive oil

- 1 Red onion, diced

- 1 teaspoon Sea salt

Directions:

1. Apply the olive oil, red onion, and salt to the skillet and cook over medium heat for around 5 minutes until the onions are tender. Add the rubbed ginger and minced garlic and simmer for a minute before applying all the spices to the mixture. Cook until the spices are fragrant, for an extra two minutes. Keep a close watch on the herbs, continually stirring to prevent fire.

2. In the skillet, stir the tomato passata or puree and allow it to continue cooking for about ten to fifteen minutes until thickened and reduced.

3. Connect the tofu and canned coconut milk to the skillet and carry the pan to a boil. Reduce the stove to low and give 10 minutes for the tikka masala to simmer. Over brown rice or buckwheat, serve wet.

50. Spicy Garlic Soba Noodles with Bok Choy

(Ready in about 40 minutes | Serving 2-4 | Difficulty: Normal)

Per serving: Kcal 315, Fat: 20g, Net Carbs: 30g, Protein: 17g

Ingredients:

- 6 ounces Soba noodles
- 6 ounces Baby bok choy
- 1 cup Bean sprouts
- 3 Green onions, diced, white and greens separated
- 3 cloves Garlic, minced
- 3 teaspoons Sesame seed oil, divided
- 2 tablespoons Tahini paste
- 1 tablespoon Rice wine vinegar
- 1 tablespoon Chili garlic sauce
- 1 tablespoon Sriracha sauce
- Tamari sauce 3 tablespoons

- .25 cup Peanuts, roasted, chopped

- .25 teaspoon Red pepper, flakes

Directions:

1. Mix the tahini paste, tamari sauce, chili garlic sauce, sriracha sauce, red wine vinegar and two teaspoons of sesame seed oil to make a soba sauce a dish. Set the sauce aside after mixing.

2. Put to a boil a large steel pot of water. When heated, add the soba noodles to the pot and cook for about seven minutes, until tender. Drain the boiling water and use cold water to drain the noodles.

3. While the noodles are frying, prepare the bok choy by adding it along with the sesame seed oil and red pepper flakes to a large skillet. While tossing regularly, cook over medium-high heat until the bok choy has started to wilt. Remove and set aside the bok choy from the pan.

4. Apply the whites of the green onions and the garlic to the skillet and simmer until fragrant for thirty seconds.

5. Pour the bean sprouts and half the prepared sauce with the onion and garlic into the skillet and cook for an extra thirty seconds.

6. Lower the heat to medium-low and add the remaining sauce and noodles that have been fried. Toss in the garlic sauce until the soba noodles are coated, then add the bok choy back to the pan and continue to cook until all the ingredients are heated through.

7. Cover the dish with the onion and peanut greens before eating.

Conclusion

Because the Dr Sebi diet strictly reduces or eliminates entire categories of foods, you may be deficient in essential nutrients such as iron, calcium, vitamin D, vitamin B12, and omega-3 fatty acids unless you plan your daily diet very carefully and consume dietary supplements regularly. Dr Sebi claims that his diet works because it is not germs that cause illness and infection, but a buildup of mucus that can only be rectified by his advised alkaline plan. There is no research to support the idea that mucus cleansing cures disease, and Dr Sebi, who has not received medical training, offers no clinical trial results, only anecdotal evidence. Even if he starts the plan, it may be difficult to keep him around friends or family members who don't have the same dietary restrictions.